TRAVELIN' AMERICA in Appliqué

Suitcase, map, scissors, thread — check your packing list, because it's time for a quilting trip through America. Travel the Fantastic 50 on this entertaining tour with designer Ursula Michael, and you'll soon be recreating your favorite regional images in appliqué. Ursula's patterns and fun "travelogue" will help you capture in fabric all the wonders of a great nation, from a towering city skyline to coyotes howling in the moonlight. Choose your favorite blocks to create any number of decorative items — whether quilts, tote bags, wall hangings, or table runners — and let your imagination be your guide through this collection of all-American appliqué.

LEISURE ARTS, INC.
Little Rock, Arkansas

Mountain STATES

Texas RANCH

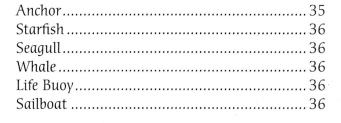

East Coast
Life by the Sea

Crisp, Cold ALASKA

Autumn in
NEW ENGLAND

Big CITYSCAPE

Heartland
FARMER'S MARKET

Old Southern
GASLIGHTS AT SUNSET

Florida
SUNSHINE

Midwest FARM LIFE

Downtown WINDOWS

Southwest DESERT

Hawaiian ISLANDS

California FUN

The Spirit of AMERICA

Travel PLANS

The appliqué patterns in this book are designed for 10" blocks. For 12" blocks, set photocopier at 120%. For 8" blocks, set photocopier at 80%.

Some patterns include dashed lines. These lines indicate individual shapes that are partially covered by other shapes.

SHOPPING FOR YOUR TRIP

Choose high-quality, medium-weight 100% cotton fabrics for your appliqués. All-cotton fabrics fray less than cotton/polyester blends.

Consider color and value (light and dark) when selecting your fabrics. You will want your appliqués to "pop" against the background and you will also want each appliqué shape within a block to be visible.

Also, consider the scale of fabric prints. A variety of large, medium, and small prints will make your designs more interesting and fun. Add some solid fabrics to the mix.

Wash, dry, and press your fabrics to shrink and remove excess dye before cutting. If you remove your fabric from the dryer while it is still slightly damp and press it dry immediately, you will find that pressing is much easier.

MODE OF TRANSPORTATION

Do you want a slow, leisurely trip? Needle-turn appliqué is for you. Or do you want to get there fast? Fusible appliqué will speed up your journey.

NEEDLE-TURN APPLIQUÉ

Packing List

> template plastic
> permanent fine-point pen
> mechanical pencil with very fine lead
> sharp scissors for cutting fabric
> scissors for cutting template plastic

Road Map

> To make templates from a pattern, use a permanent pen to carefully trace each shape of the pattern onto template plastic. Cut out templates along drawn lines. Check templates against the original pattern for accuracy.

> Place a template on the right side of fabric. Use mechanical pencil to draw around the template onto your fabric. Use scissors to cut out appliqué shape approximately $3/16$" outside drawn line.

> Arrange appliqué shapes onto background and pin or baste in place and needle-turn appliqué.

FUSIBLE APPLIQUÉ

Packing List

    paper-backed fusible web
    plain white paper
    black fine-point marker
    pencil
    sharp scissors for cutting fabric

Flight Plan

Patterns need to be reversed for fusible appliqué. To reverse patterns, use a black fine-point marker to trace the pattern onto plain white paper. Turn paper over and use the wrong side as your pattern.

Shapes that appear "behind" other shapes should "underlap" or extend underneath the other shapes. While tracing and cutting these shapes, add approximately $1/4$" underlaps. This will prevent gaps between shapes and will make the appliqué design smoother.

Place paper-backed fusible web, web side down, over pattern. Use a pencil to trace each shape of the pattern, including any needed underlaps, onto paper side of web, leaving at least $1/2$" between shapes.

To reduce stiffness of larger appliqué shapes, cut away the center of the fusible web $1/4$" inside the traced line. Do not cut on the line.

White or light-colored fabrics may need to be lined with fusible interfacing before applying fusible web to prevent darker fabrics from showing through.

Follow manufacturer's instructions to fuse traced shapes to wrong side of fabrics. Do not remove paper backing.

Cut out appliqué shapes along traced lines. Remove paper backing from all shapes.

For wall hangings or decorative pillows that will not receive wear and will not be laundered, you may choose to simply fuse your appliqués. For more permanent appliqués, you may machine stitch around all exposed edges of your appliqués using a zigzag, Satin Stitch, Blanket Stitch, or other decorative stitch your machine offers. Or, if you prefer, you may hand Blanket Stitch edges of appliqués.

Popular DESTINATIONS

As you begin appliquéing, you may decide to make one block or all one hundred! Here are some project ideas to inspire you.

For a small space on your wall, use three blocks in a row. Use more blocks to make just the right size wall hanging.

A throw is a perfect gift for a traveling companion. Use 12 or so blocks that reflect a past vacation together. Maybe you can even find some novelty prints that repeat the theme of your appliqués.

Combine 20 or more blocks to make a quilt for your bed for reminiscing over past vacations or dreaming of future adventures. Make a coordinating pillow from your favorite block.

Add setting triangles to your finished blocks for an octagon shaped quilt to use as a table topper. Make coordinating place mats, all alike or with different blocks. (Wouldn't blocks inspired by the Hawaiian Islands be fun for a Luau? How about a Texas Ranch table runner for your next barbecue?)

Make your own tote using a block, or simply appliqué a design onto a purchased cloth tote. Ursula made hers using the Flip-Flop pattern for a beach bag, but you can personalize yours for your next vacation.

Bison   page 20

Mountain STATES

The Rocky Mountains reach up toward the sky with a strength and life that's all their own. As you wind through the Rockies, you will truly witness nature's grandeur. In the stillness of a moonlit night, stop to rest under the colossal trees and listen to the sounds of nature. Batiks in deep, rich colors are perfect for replicating these majestic mountain sights.

Single Pine Cone   page 21

Bull Moose   page 22

Log Cabin page 23

Tall Trees page 26

Bear page 24

Purple Mountains page 27

Pine Cones page 25

Coyote page 28

19

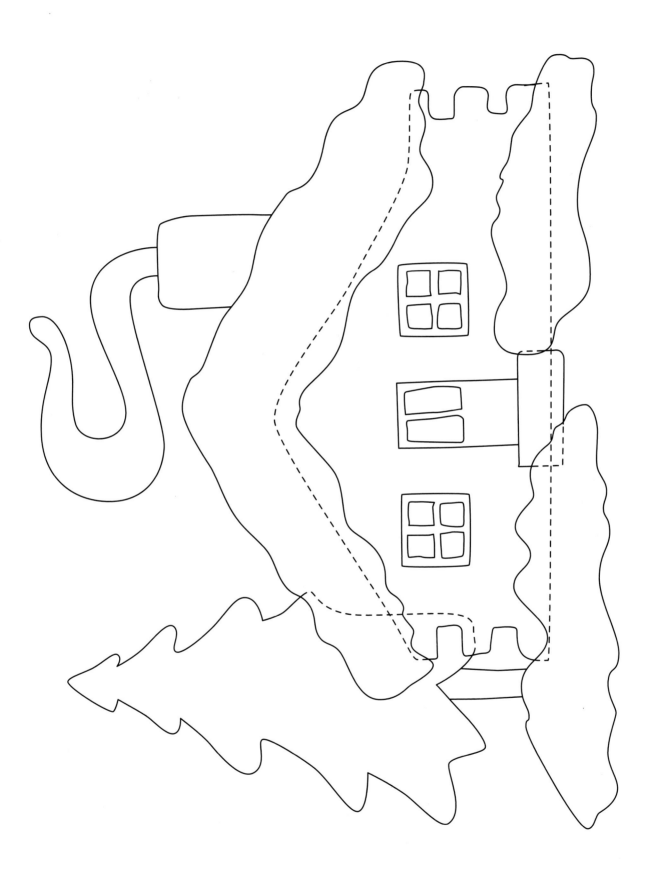

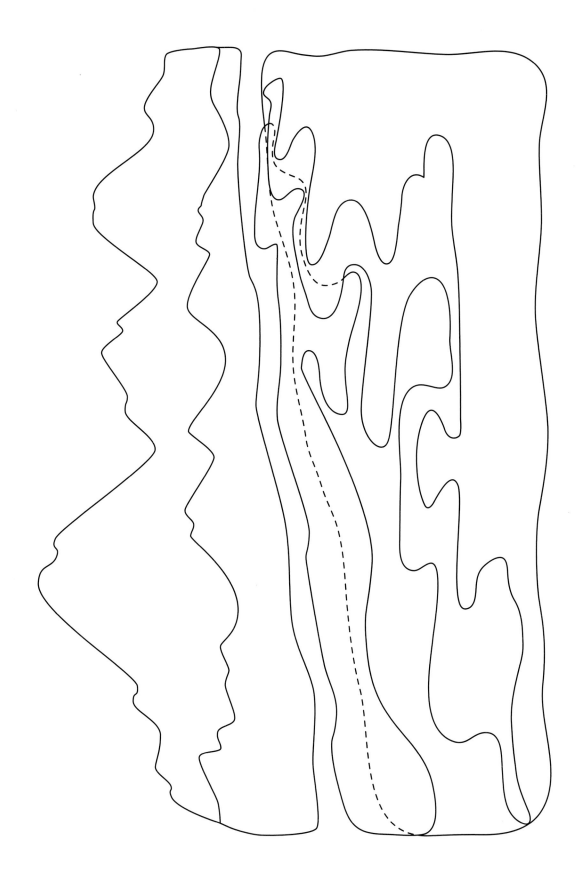

Horseshoe page 30

Hat page 31

Boot page 32

Texas RANCH

That's right, pardner! Everything in the Lone Star State is bigger and better! Be sure to take plenty of snacks and drinks if you're driving, because the ranches and the roads seem to go on forever. Earth-tone plaids are just right for a Texas-style banner or throw pillow. And western prints in all colors and patterns will make a great quilt with rows of boots for your little cowboy.

Lone Star page 33

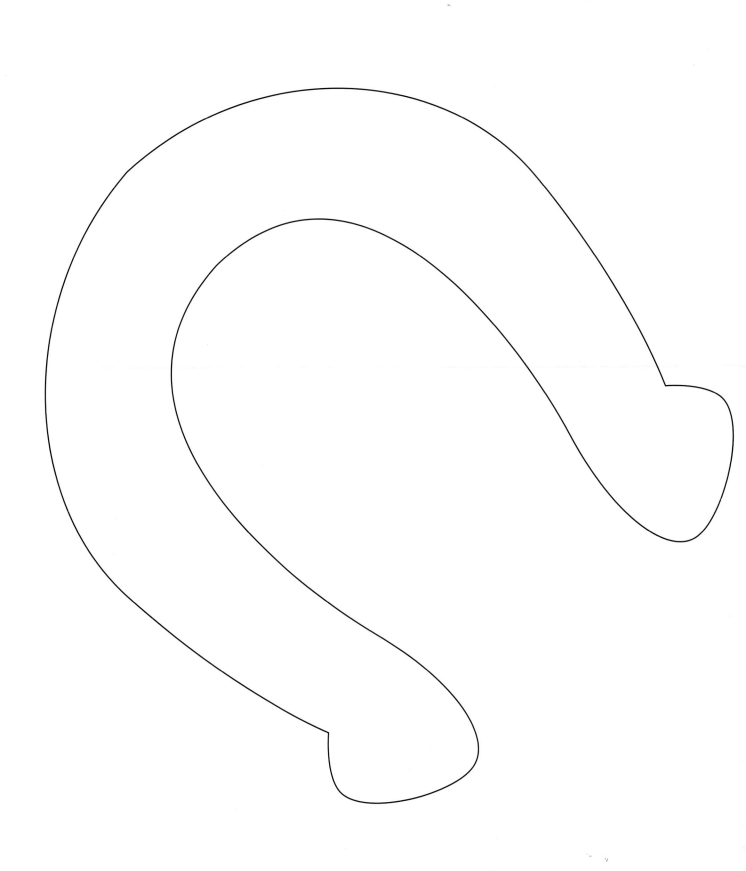

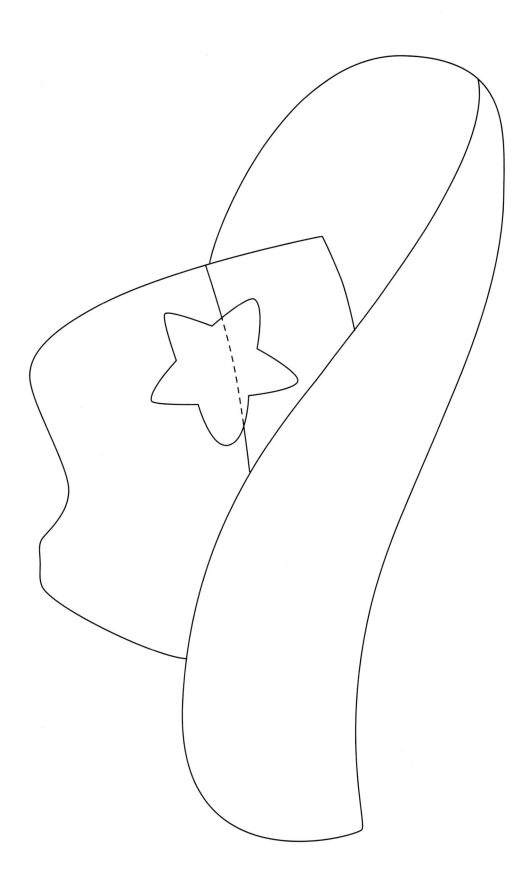

Sea Horse   page 37

Lighthouse   page 39

Sand Dollar   page 40

Fish   page 38

Scallop Shell   page 41

East Coast
Life by the Sea

Take a slow walk along the sandy beaches of the east coast, a red bucket in your hand, your footprints washing away by the rolling waves as you look for the treasures deposited by the morning's high tide. The ocean spray mingles with the calling of the gulls. Every breath you take brings you deeper relaxation. Let your search for serenity lead you to your favorite fabric store, where you'll find the perfect hues of aqua, blue, and green.

Crab   page 42

Anchor   page 43

Whale page 46

Starfish page 44

Life Buoy page 47

Seagull page 45

Sailboat page 48

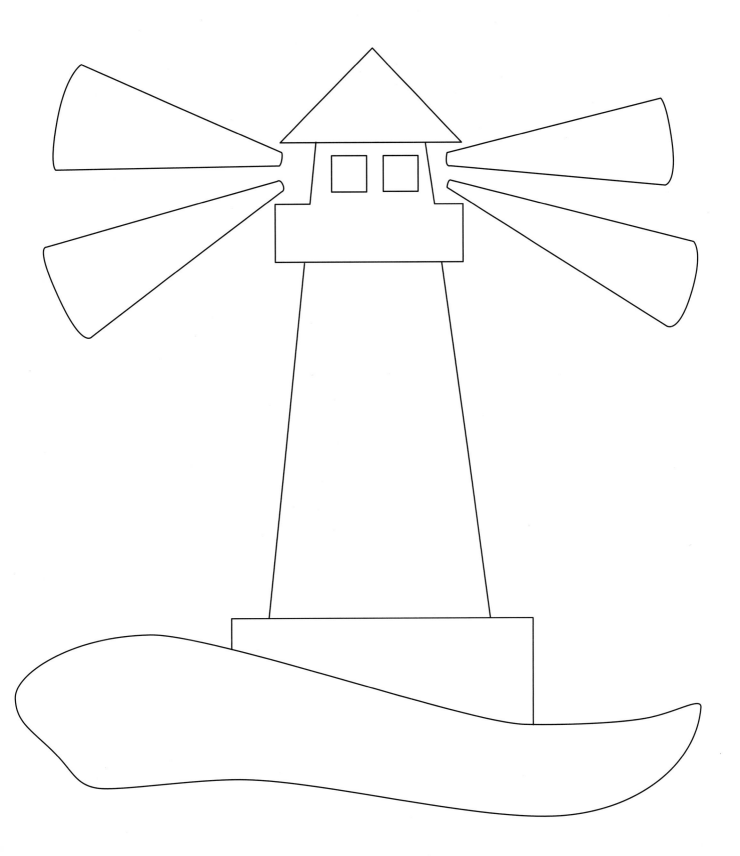

40

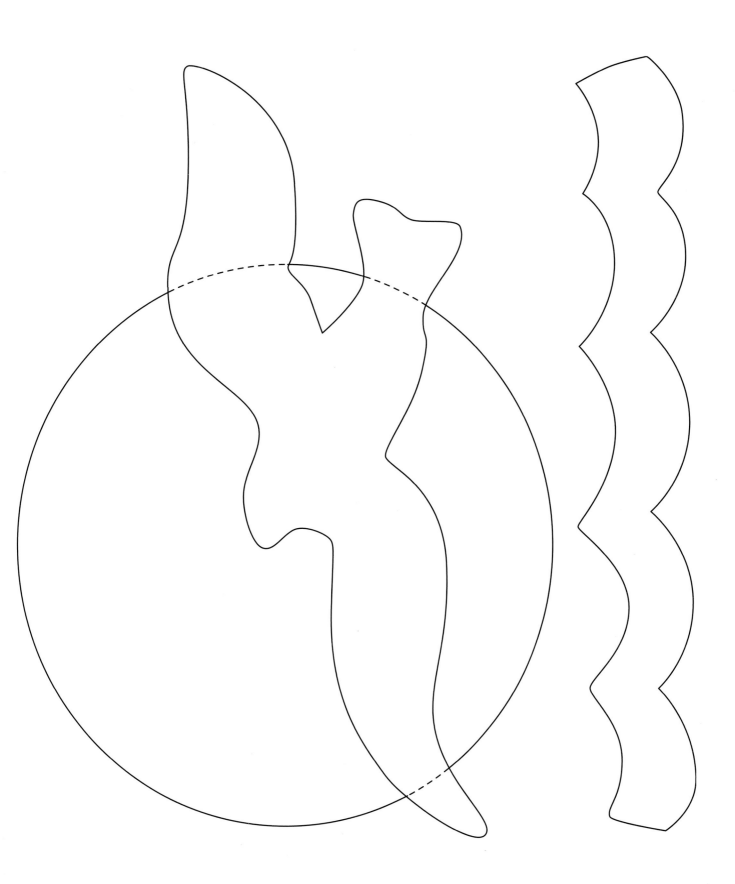

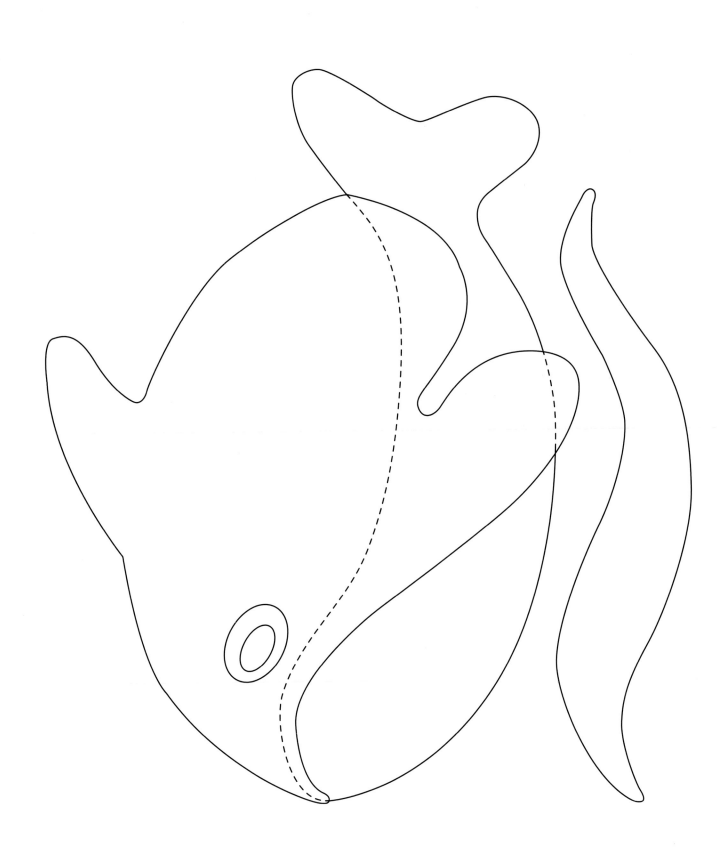

48

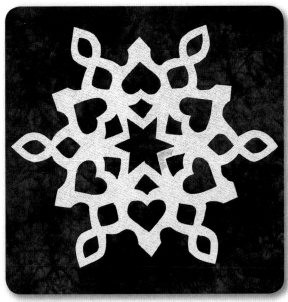

Sleigh   page 50

Tree   page 51

Crisp, Cold ALASKA

Wind, snow, and bone-chilling cold will add to your adventures in Alaska. Here you will find rugged individuals offering easy welcomes and warm hearts. Try stark white appliqués against a dark blue background. A snowflake print will be perfect for sashings and borders to frame your wintry blocks.

Holly   page 53

Snowflake   page 52

Apple Basket   *page 56*

Autumn in NEW ENGLAND

Visiting new England in September or October, you will experience the dazzling colors of the landscape. Trees spread a blanket of vivid reds, greens, and yellows over the hills and into quaint villages and farms. Stroll around a town square and explore the historical churches, antique shops, and restored homes. Drive down a New England country lane and you'll find farm stands that beckon with baskets of fresh apples and bouquets of dried herbs—and there's sure to be an old wagon or two loaded with an assortment of pumpkins. Fabrics in a spectrum of fall colors capture the refreshing spirit of autumn.

Tree and Moon at Night   *page 57*

Pumpkin   *page 58*

Maple Leaves   page 59

Antiqué Shop   page 62

Red Barn   page 60

Trees and Stars at Night   page 63

Home   page 61

White Church   page 64

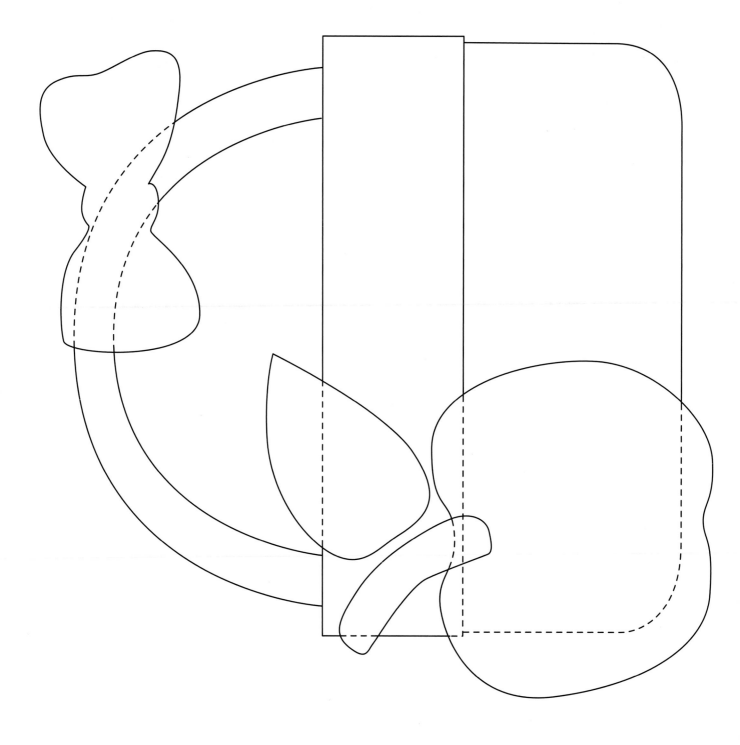

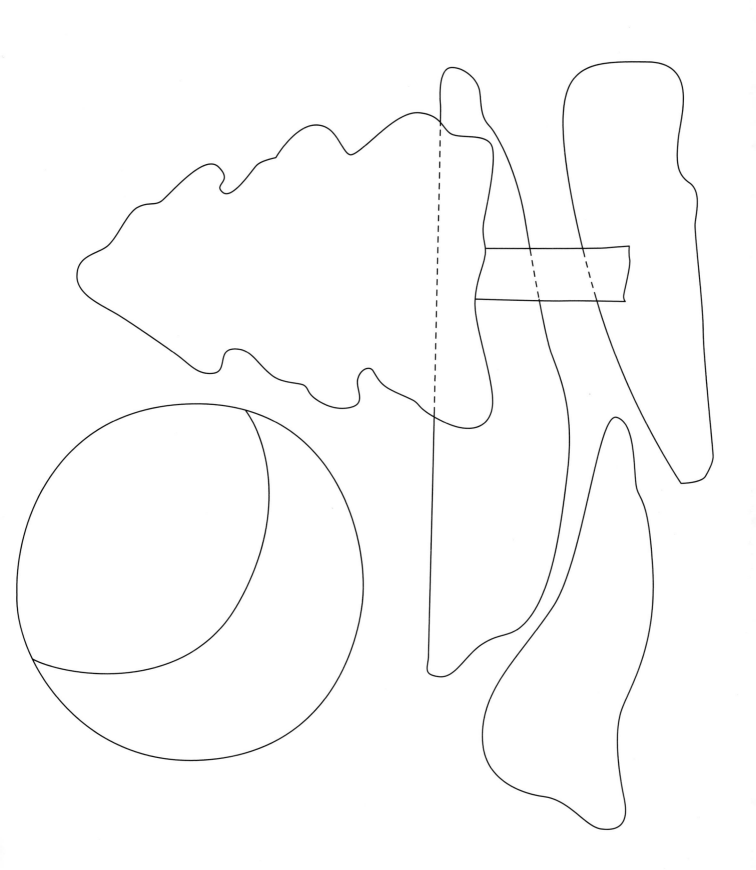

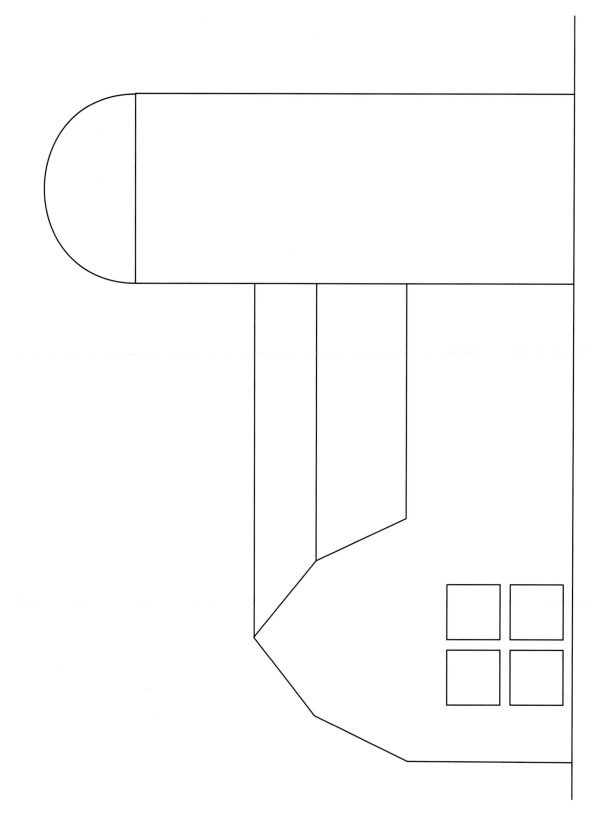

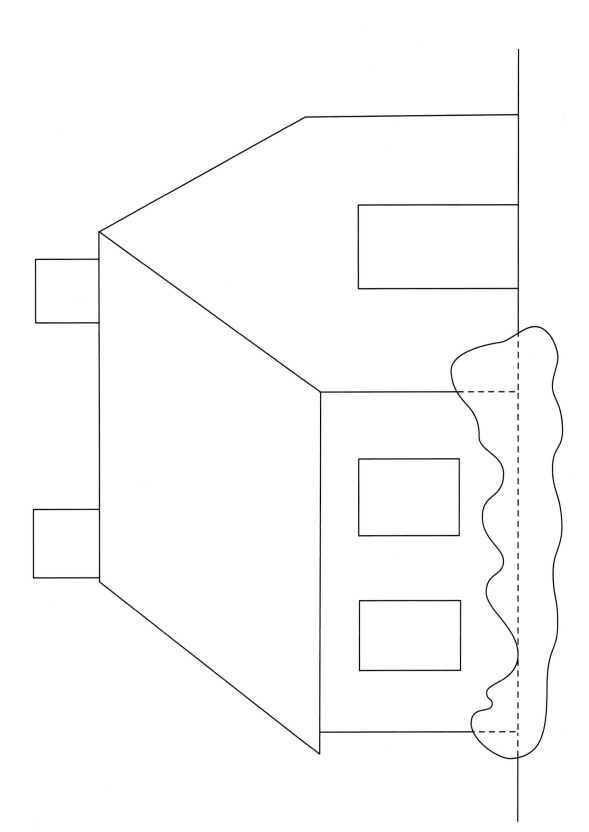

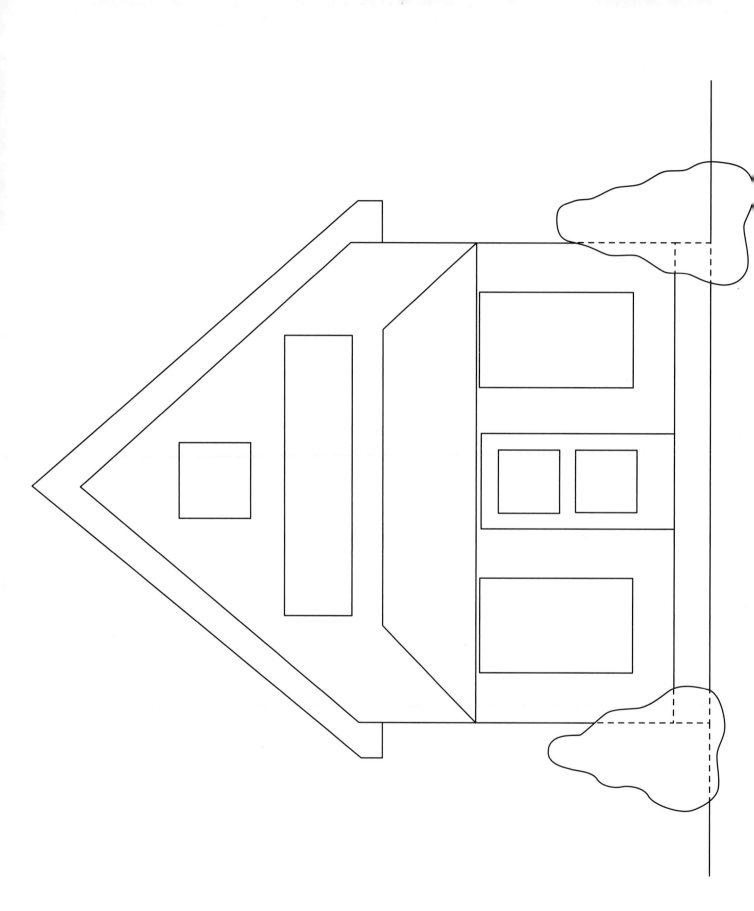

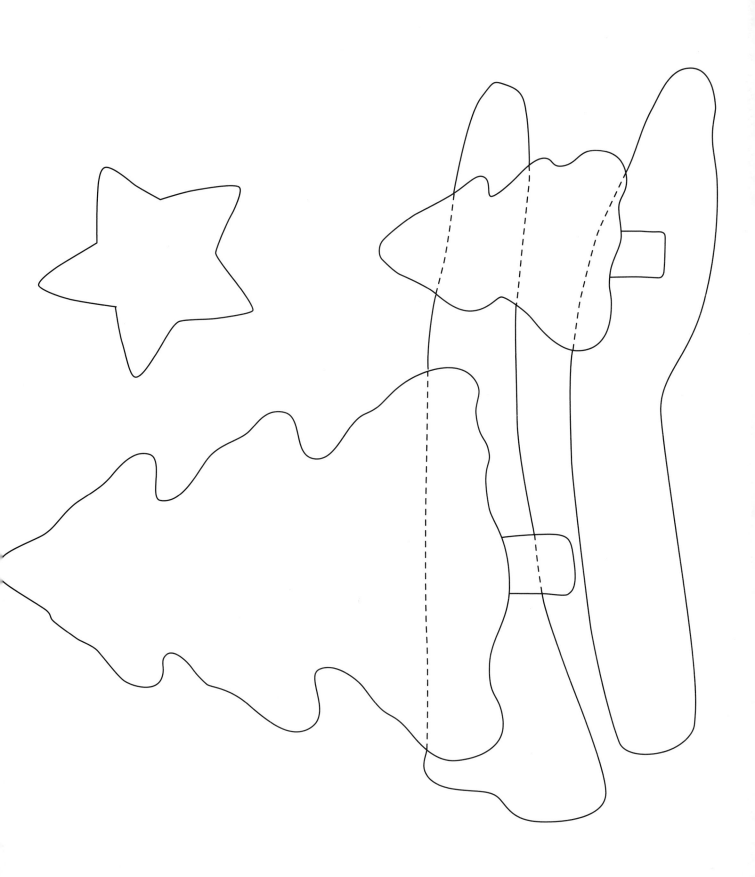

Cityscape #1   page 66

Big
CITYSCAPE

Cityscape #2   page 67

Cityscape #3   page 68

The energy of the city draws you in, tempting you to endlessly explore the culture of each neighborhood. You stare in awe at the towering skyscrapers, enjoy excellent entertainment at theaters, and dine in the finest restaurants. Even though the lines of the skyline are straight and square, the textures of the buildings vary from structure to structure. An urban skyline makes a wonderful project for experimenting with light and dark fabrics.

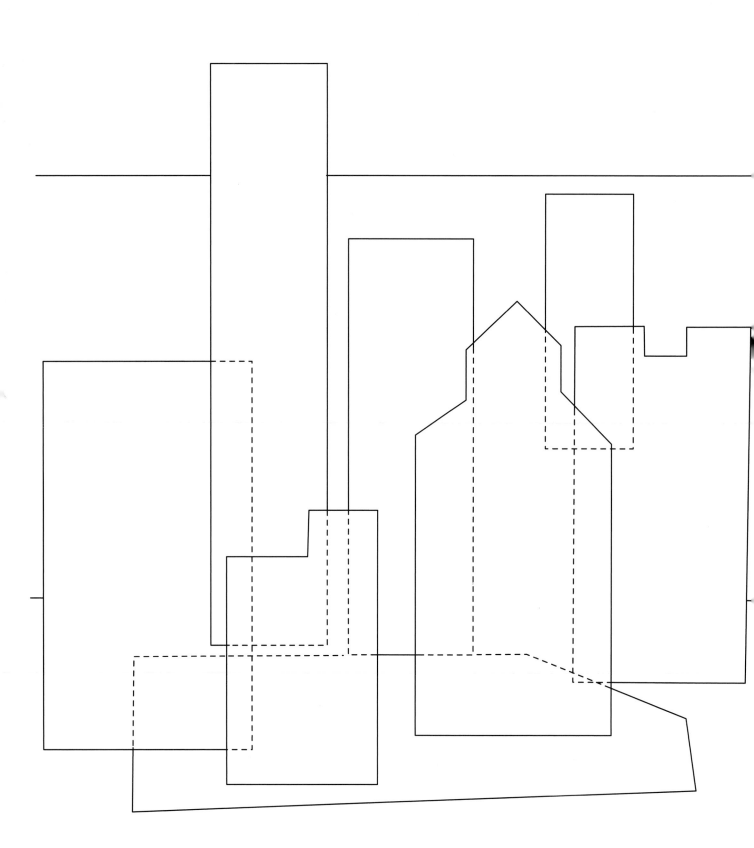

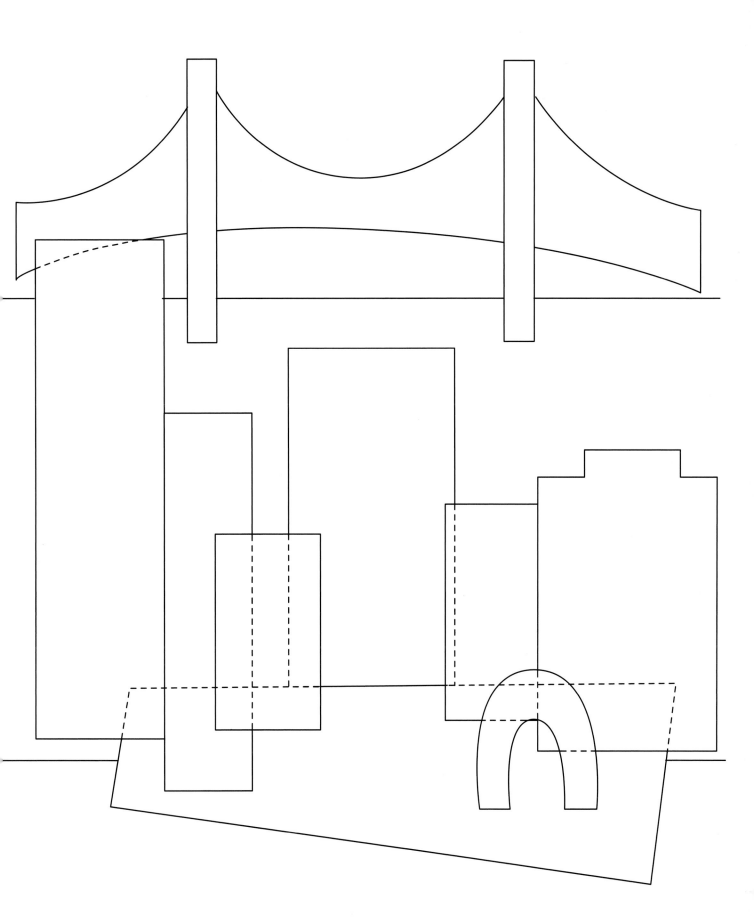

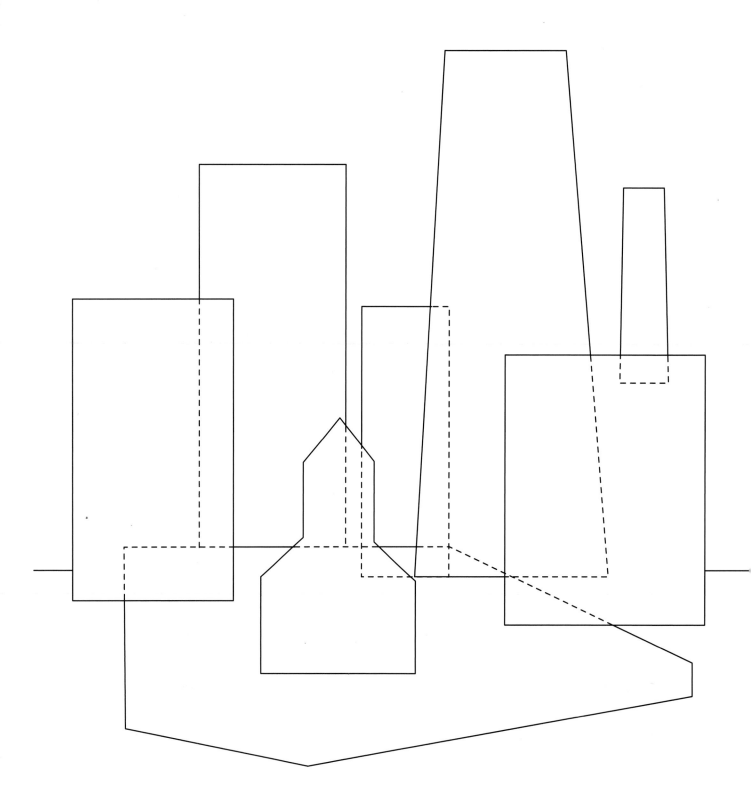

Sunflower page 71

Heartland FARMER'S MARKET

The heartland of America is a region of bountiful farms on rolling hills and fertile plains. Be sure to pause at the local farmers' markets. There you'll find trucks filled with fresh vegetables, crates of fruit, homemade bread, and handmade crafts. A wall hanging, table runner, and coordinating place mats featuring these fruit and vegetable designs will make your kitchen "market fresh."

Eggplant page 72

Watermelon page 73

Strawberries   page 74

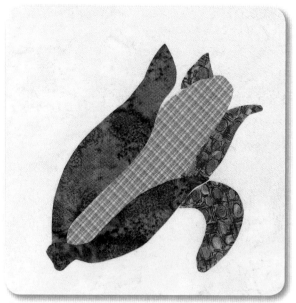

Corn   page 77

Asparagus   page 75

Peaches   page 78

Cherries   page 76

Carrots   page 79

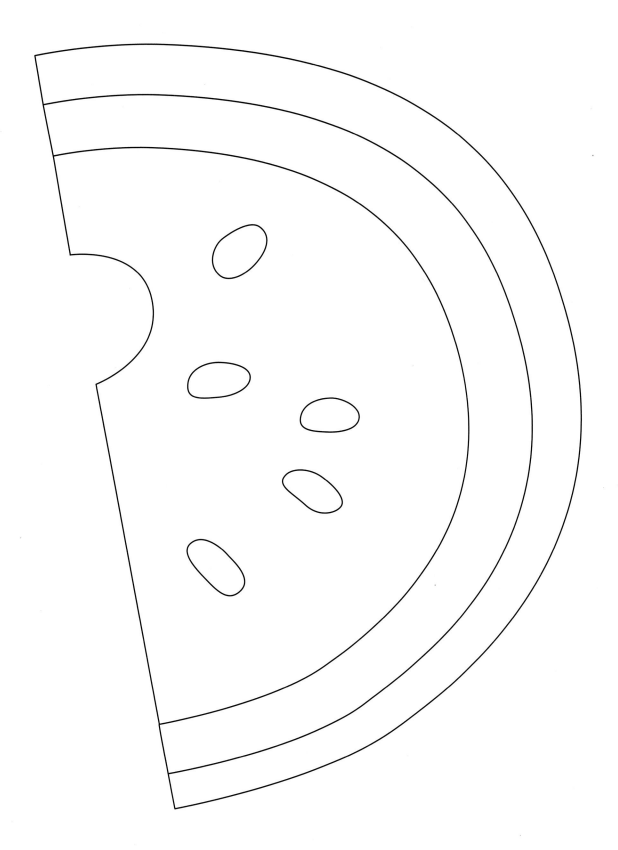

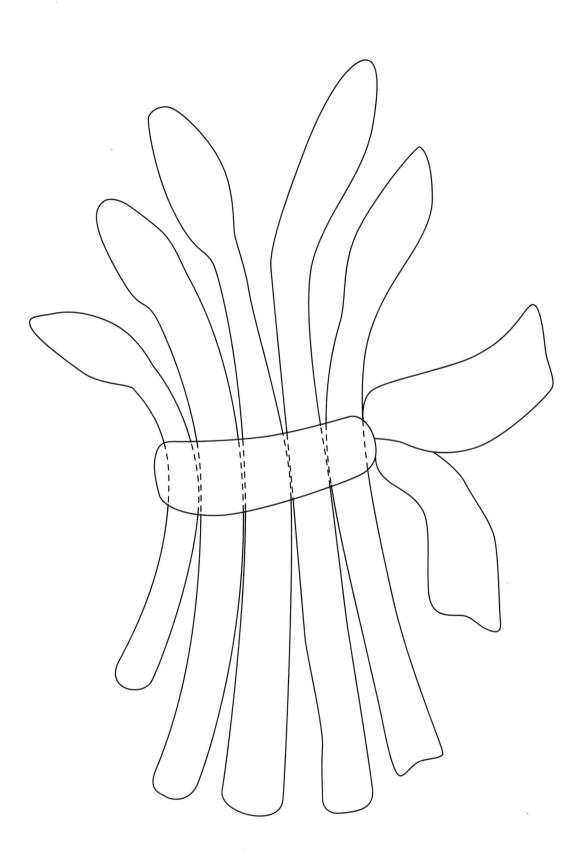

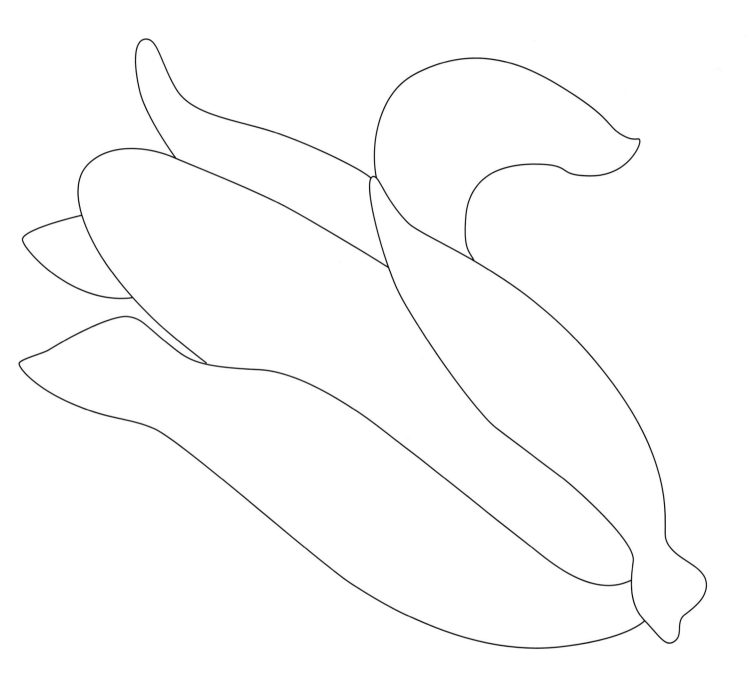

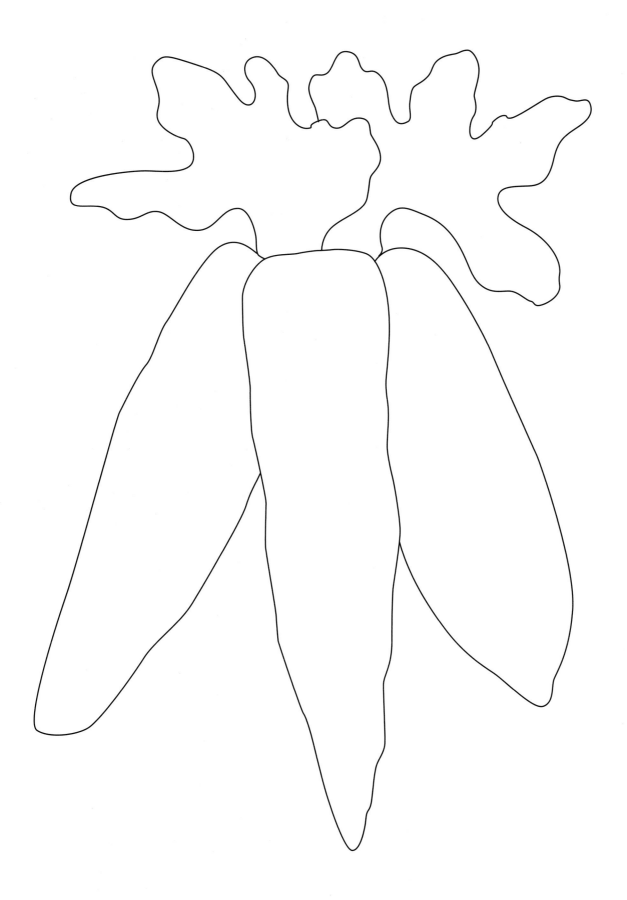

Take a stroll along a brick walkway on a sultry summer evening in an old southern town. Dark iron fences surround the manicured lawns and fountains gurgle in rose garden parks. The wrought iron gaslights are lit, casting shadows on the uneven pavement. A fabric with a tie-dyed or hand painted look makes black appliqué lamps glow.

Gaslight #1   page 81

Old Southern
GASLIGHTS AT SUNSET

Gaslight #2   page 82

Gaslight #3   page 83

82

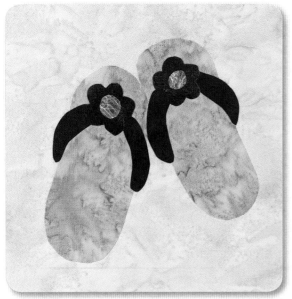

Flip-Flops   page 86

Sunshine   page 88

Kite   page 87

Beach Umbrella   page 89

Florida SUNSHINE

Discover the carefree life in Florida! Relax on the beach, roam through a salt marsh, and indulge in people-watching under the bright sunshine. Bright fabrics will capture these happy days on banners and place mats. Add an appliquéd happy sun or flip-flops to a vivid T-shirt or beach bag. Use these designs to create your own place in the sun.

Beach Bag   page 90

Sun Hat   page 91

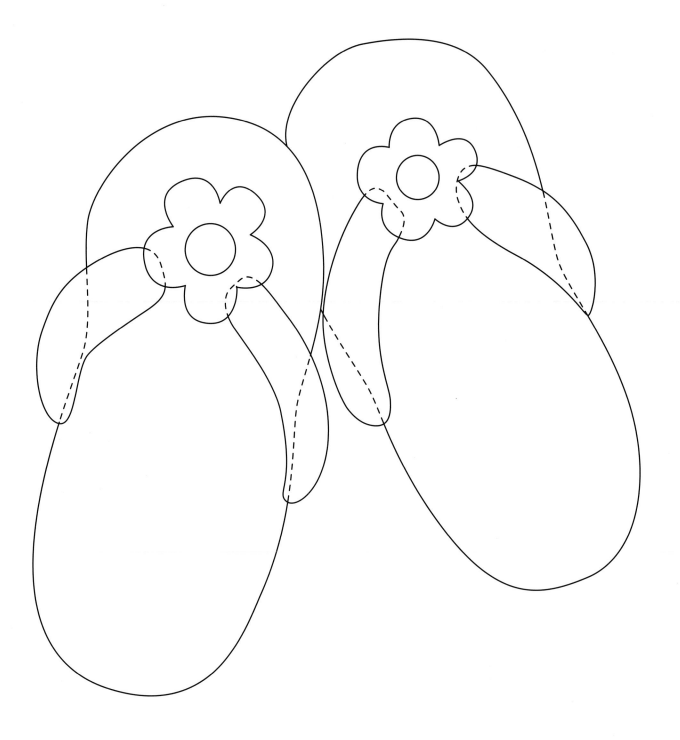

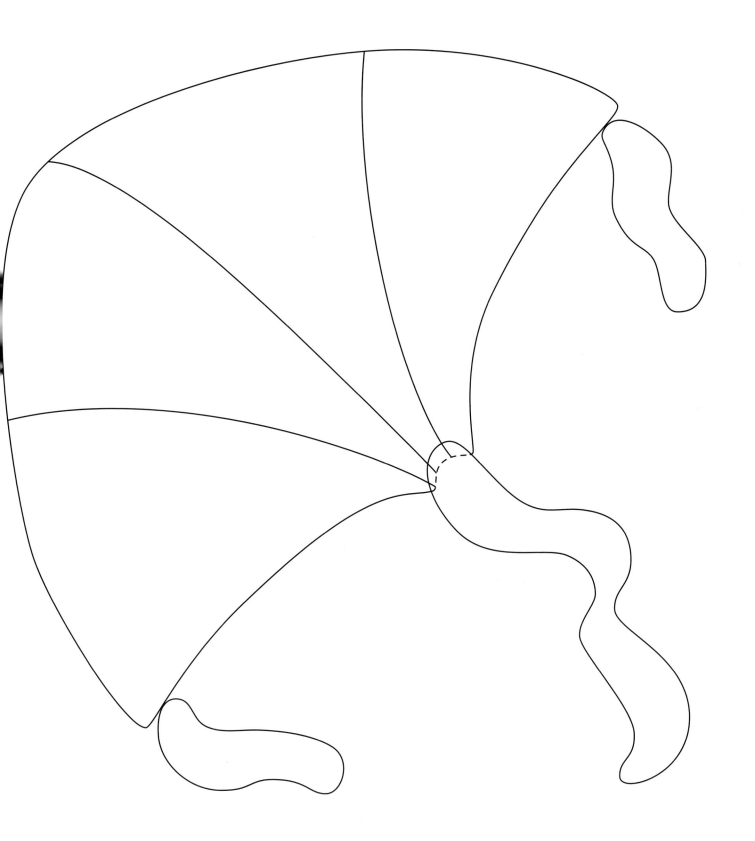

Midwest Farm Life

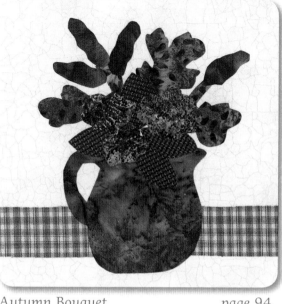

Autumn Bouquet   page 94

As your journey takes you through the friendly tangle of small towns and farms in the Midwest, you'll see countless farm animals and flower gardens. Imagine the cozy farm kitchens adorned with seasonal bouquets and wreaths of dried flowers. Make mini quilts featuring animals, flowers, or combine all the designs for a true "farm country" quilt. How about a quilt with blocks made from one animal design for that special child in your life?

Christmas Wreath   page 95

Rooster   page 96

Cow   page 97

Basket of Tulips   page 98

Sheep   page 99

Pig   page 100

Red Geraniums   page 101

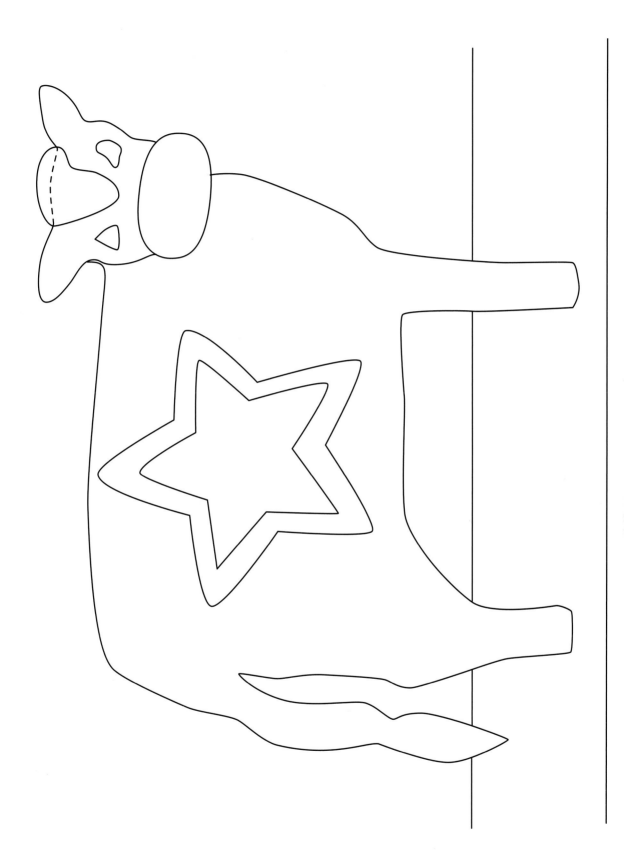

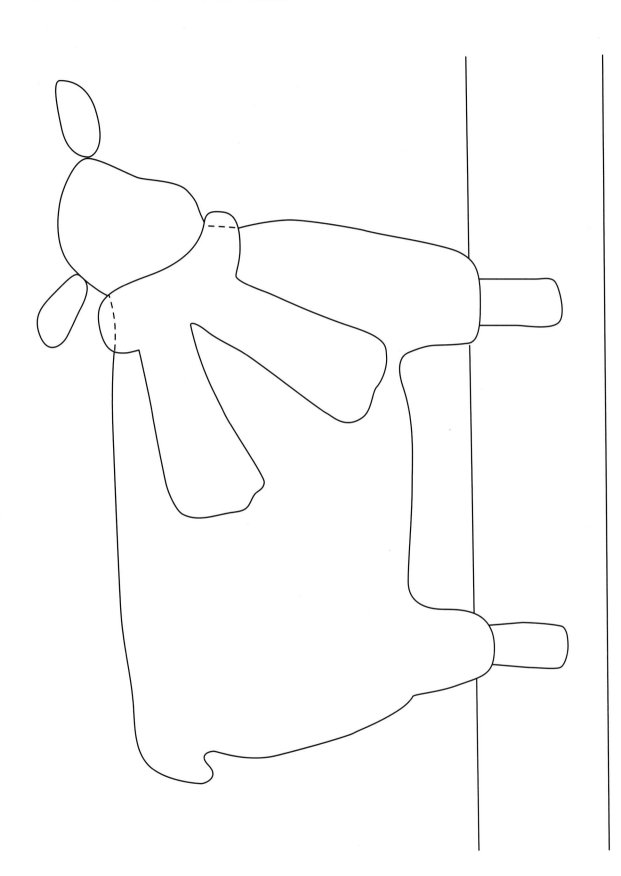

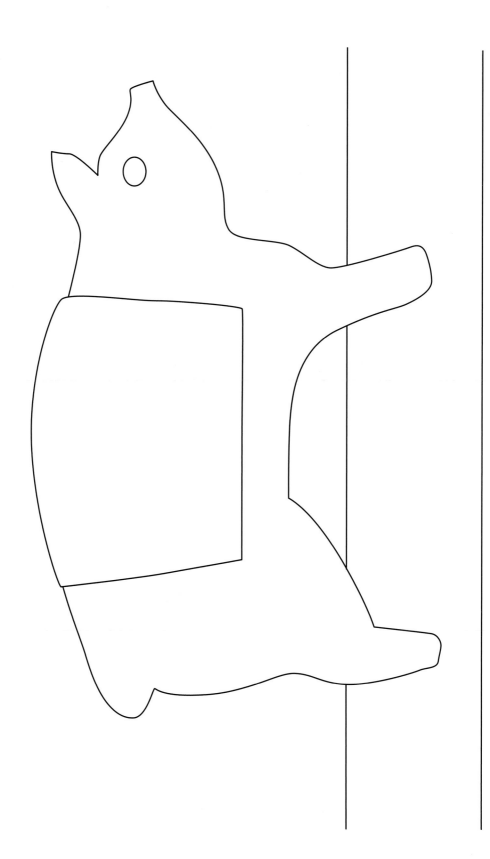

Casement Window   page 104

Dormer Window   page 107

Rectangular Window   page 105

Square Window   page 108

Arched Window with Shutters   page 106

Shuttered Window   page 109

Arched Window with Flowers   *page 110*

Downtown WINDOWS

Old downtown neighborhoods boast the most interesting architectural elements. As you meander along the cobbled streets, remember to look up at the windows of the buildings. Lovely lace curtains shift in the breeze here, unique shutters bracket an open space there, and everywhere flower boxes add splashes of color. Recreate your favorite neighborhood with stone, brick, stucco, and wood prints.

Arched Window with Curtains   *page 111*

Oval Window   *page 112*

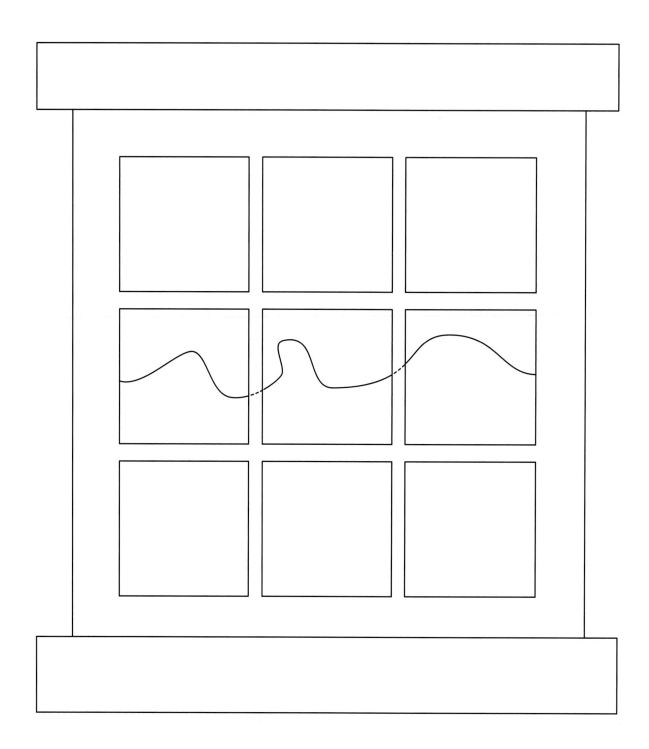

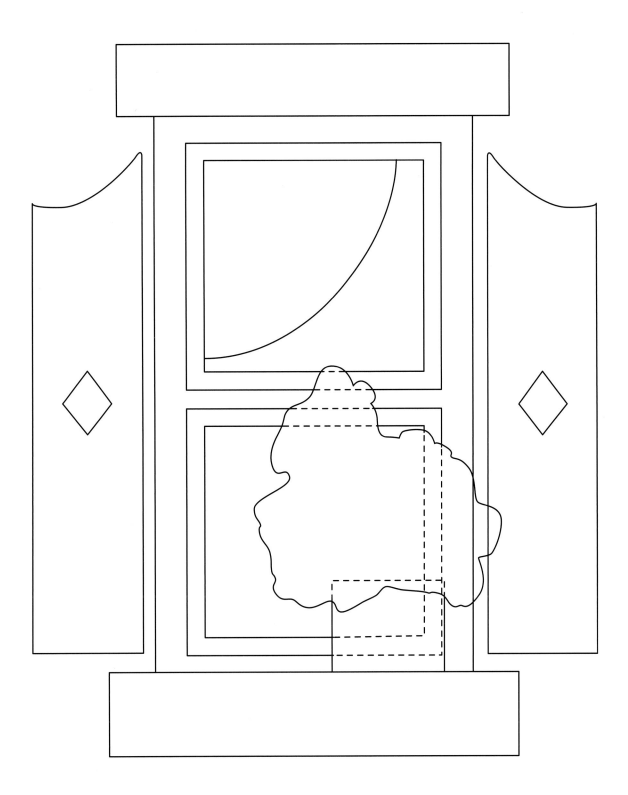

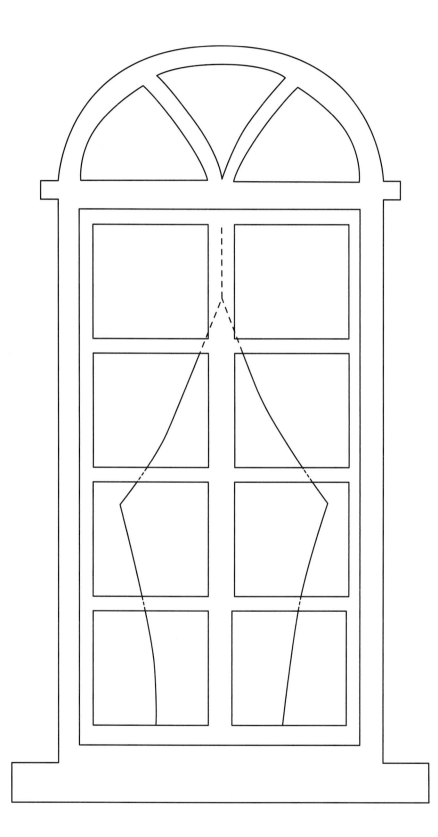

Pot with Wide Mouth   page 115

Southwest
DESERT

As you cross the southwest desert, you will be awed by the endless miles of sand and dunes. The dunes change colors every hour of the day and are black beneath a canopy of twinkling stars at night. Native Americans have stylized these incredible scenes and combined symbols of their heritage to create magnificent pottery. Let their traditional designs inspire you.

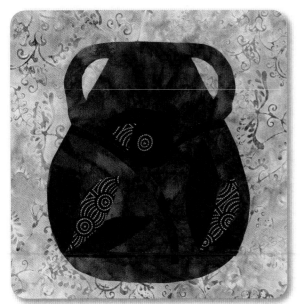

Short Pot   page 118

Pot with Handles   page 116

Pot with Fowl   page 119

Pot with Mountains   page 117

115

Hawaiian
ISLANDS

Red Ginger   page 122

Your tour across America must include the enchanting islands of Hawaii. Exotic flowers, clear blue waters, and a sky as big as the ocean—Nature creates a breathtaking backdrop for graceful native dances. Traditional Hawaiian quilt motifs and four large flowers make up these enchanting designs. Choose from the nearly limitless batiks and Hawaiian prints to make your own island treasure.

Foliage   page 123

Hibiscus   page 124

Palm Trees and Sunsets page 125

Blue Trumpet Vine page 128

Orchid page 126

Bird of Paradise page 129

Pomegranates page 127

Center Motif   page 134

Butterfly #1   page 132

Fan   page 135

Butterfly #2   page 133

Butterfly #3   page 136

Butterfly #4   page 137

California FUN

These butterfly designs symbolize the freedom of self-expression found only in California. Drive the winding roads over the mountain tops, browse in the myriad of unique shops, or sun on the beautiful beaches. You may even meet a movie star as you explore Hollywood's night life. Choose lots of bold colors to mirror the many moods of uninhibited California.

The Spirit of AMERICA

Appliqué a statement of your patriotism in red, white, and blue. It's a wonderful way to celebrate all the beauty and variety that makes our country great.

Stars and Stripes   page 141

Big Apple   page 139

America   page 142

Heart   page 140

Sailboat   page 143

Ursula Michael

Ursula Michael's work as a designer began several years ago. Her cross stitch and crochet patterns have enchanted a generation of needlework enthusiasts, while her award-winning designs also found their way onto giftware items.

And now, Ursula's fans will be delighted to know that she has returned to one of her earliest creative endeavors — quilting.

"When I got married in the '70s," says Ursula, "my mom gave me a box of fabric scraps. Included in the box were fabrics from dresses my grandmother made for me, as well as scraps from Mom's home sewing projects. Mom told me to 'do something' with those fabrics. So I made a crazy quilt. I'd never made a quilt before, so the finished quilt was heavy and bulky. Nevertheless, I still cherish that quilt. Every time I look at it, I see my childhood in those memory-filled fabrics."

Quilting still holds a special place in Ursula's heart. Through the years, she has often used quilting motifs, tucking them into her other needlework designs.

Ursula describes her quilt design style as, "a combination of traditional and contemporary motifs. I use clean, bright colors to create unique appliqué quilts."

This book of appliqué designs was inspired by Ursula's travels across the United States. She especially loves exploring village streets, back roads, mountains, rivers, and coastal regions. In fact, Ursula and her husband, Al are now settled into their dream home in Rhode Island, where Ursula is never far from a wide variety of landscapes.

Stitch along with Ursula as she shares her love of the land that inspired this charming collection of appliqués. To see more of her engaging designs, visit www. UrsulaMichael.com

EDITORIAL STAFF

Vice President and Editor-in-Chief: Sandra Graham Case
Executive Director of Publications: Cheryl Nodine Gunnells
Senior Director of Publications: Susan White Sullivan
Director of Designer Relations: Debra Nettles
Art Operations Director: Jeff Curtis
Art Publications Director: Rhonda Hodge Shelby
Art Imaging Director: Mark Hawkins
Publication Operations Director: Cheryl Johnson
Technical Editor: Lisa Lancaster
Technical Writer: Frances Huddleston
Editorial Writer: Susan McManus Johnson
Senior Graphic Artist: Lora Puls
Imaging Technician: Mark R. Potter
Photography Stylist: Jan Nobles
Publishing Systems Administrator: Becky Riddle
Publishing Systems Assistants: Clint Hanson, Josh Hyatt, and John Rose

Contributing Photographers: Jerry Davis and Ken West

BUSINESS STAFF

Chief Operating Officer: Tom Siebenmorgen
Vice President, Sales and Marketing: Pam Stebbins
Director of Sales and Services: Margaret Reinold
Vice President, Operations: Jim Dittrich
Comptroller, Operations: Rob Thieme
Retail Customer Service Managers: Stan Raynor
Print Production Manager: Fred F. Pruss